The Pinky Promise

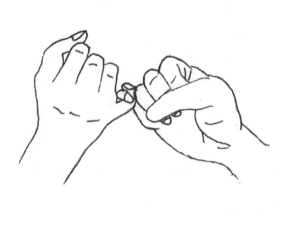

by Sailesh Rao

Illustrations by Kimaya Rao,
Roxanne Chappell and Niharika Desiraju

ISBN: 9798372180895

"The wise hear and see as little children do."

- Lao Tzu

Unity Stew

Table of Contents

About the Author and Illustrators

Sailesh Rao, Kimaya Rao, Roxanne Chappell and
Niharika Desiraju

Sailesh Rao is the Founder and Executive Director of Climate Healers, a non-profit dedicated towards healing the Earth's climate. He is a systems engineer, Human, Earth and Animal Liberation (HEAL) activist, husband, dad and since 2010, a star-struck grandfather. *The Pinky Promise* recounts how and why he promised his grand-daughter, Kimaya, that the world will be largely Vegan before she turns 16 in 2026, so that people will stop eating her relatives, the animals. He has faith that humanity will transform to keep his pinky promise to Kimaya, not just for ethical reasons, but also out of sheer ecological necessity. He has created a Climate Bathtub model to help humanity understand the solution space for enabling a thriving planet and reversing climate change, which clearly shows the ecological necessity for realizing a Vegan World as soon as possible and certainly before 2026.

Kimaya Rao is in sixth grade at a Montessori School in Phoenix, AZ and she is the primary illustrator for the book. She loves art, volleyball and spending time with her friends and family, including three cats—Miss Ruka, Freddy and Miro—and a bunny rabbit, Almond. Her mother, Roxanne Chappell, contributed four of the illustrations including the cover art, while the Wishing Tree illustration was contributed by Niharika Desiraju for *Carbon Dharma: The Occupation of Butterflies*.

"As we return to our true childlike nature of awe and wonder, we will remember how to love our earth family and heal the damage we have done."

- Judy McCoy Carman

Prologue

By Judy McCoy Carman, M.A.

This is the story of a devoted grandfather, Sailesh Rao; the wisdom he learned from his beloved granddaughter, Kimaya; and the promise he made to her to do his part to save the world and those who live here. His vow to her reminded me of a song written by John Denver. John sings in "Rhymes and Reasons,"

"It is here we must begin to seek the wisdom of the children
and the graceful way of flowers in the wind.
For the children and the flowers are my sisters and my brothers,
their laughter and their loveliness could clear a cloudy day.
Like the music of the mountain and the colors of the rainbow,
they're a promise of the future and a blessing for today.

Though the cities start to crumble and the towers fall around us,
The sun is slowly fading and it's colder than the sea.
It is written: From the desert to the mountains they shall lead us,
By the hand and by the heart, they will comfort you and me.
In their innocence and trusting they will teach us to be free.
For the children and the flowers are my sisters and my brothers,
Their laughter and their loveliness could clear a cloudy day,
And the song that I am singing is a prayer to non-believers,
Come and stand beside us. We can find a better way."

If you are noticing the destruction taking place all around us—the ravages caused by animal agriculture to the seas, the forests, the land, the precious air we breathe, the extinction of wild animals, along with massive starvation and disease around the world—this story of a grandfather's love and willingness to listen to the wisdom of a child will give you the faith and reason for action that you need.

This book is truly a sacred and powerful prayer to "come and stand beside us" and "find a better way." We adults have lived as Homo Sapiens too long, believing that we could dominate, exploit and, yes, kill whomever appears to be in the way. But by listening to his granddaughter, Kimaya, Sailesh is here with her pointing us to the "greatest transformation in human history."

As we open our hearts to the innocence and pure love of children, we learn, as Kimaya knows, "all life is one family," and we don't use or eat anyone in our family. The transformation of humanity from Homo Sapiens to Homo Ahimsa[1] is essential if we are to find our true nature as partners with, not dominators of, all life. We are not here to destroy life as we have been doing, but rather to embrace and adore and celebrate life. As we return to our true childlike nature of awe and wonder, we will remember how to love our earth family and heal the damage we have done. May we all commit, in our own unique ways, to a Pinky Promise with all the children of earth. May we find our true path to our highest nature as the loving human, Homo Ahimsa.[2] May all beings be happy. May all beings be free.

—

Notes:
1. "Ahimsa" is the Sanskrit word for "non-harm." Its broader meaning includes lovingkindness, nonviolence, and compassion for all earthlings. Mahatma Gandhi took a vow of ahimsa. His nonviolent resistance, based on ahimsa values and "truth force," inspired the world.

2. "Homo Ahimsa" is our true nature. It is described in the books Peace to All Beings and Homo Ahimsa. A clear vision of it is seen on manifesto - Climate Healers which states, "We imagine a world in which people can put on their Chrysalis avatars to leave their Caterpillar past behind and join together as true equals but each with unique gifts in a cooperative effort to depollute and regenerate the Earth in preparation for the birth of the Butterfly (Homo Ahimsa) stage of humanity."

*This prologue is offered with deep respect and gratitude to Kimaya and Sailesh by Judy McCoy Carman, M.A., Author: **Homo Ahimsa: Who we Really are and how we're going to save the world** and **Peace to All Beings: Veggie Soup for the Chicken's Soul** (peacetoallbeings. com); Interfaith Vegan Coalition (idausa.org)*

The most amazing

Chapter 1

The Most Amazing Thing

I came home that December night in 2005, dog tired, plopped down on the sofa and turned on the TV. There was Vice President Al Gore talking about global warming to some activists in San Francisco. I was rooted to my seat, filled with horror and I told my wife, Jaine, that if half of what he is saying is true, I feel like I'm wasting my time working on making the internet even ten times faster. She said that if you think it is that important, why don't you look into it.

That's what I did.

Within three months, I realized that it was far worse than what Mr. Gore was saying. He was only looking at the impact of our energy demands on the planet, while neglecting our food and other consumer demands. Nevertheless, I wrote to Mr. Gore offering to be of help with his mission and got trained by him in Nashville in November of 2006. As part of this training, I had agreed to give his presentation at least ten times in a year.

Once I fulfilled my obligation, I founded the non-profit, Climate Healers in December of 2007. The goal of Climate Healers is to heal the climate as opposed to maintaining it in a high state of disrepair as the mainstream environmental community, including Mr. Gore, was framing it. They didn't want to touch the third rail of environmentalism

- our culture of consumerism, especially of animal foods. To give you an analogy, imagine that you have a lump the size of a coconut by the side of your head and a 1 degree Celsius fever to go with it. You go to the doctor and the doctor says,

"I'll make sure that your fever doesn't go over 2 degrees Celsius while you develop a second lump the size of a coconut on the other side of your head."

Wouldn't you think that this doctor is crazy and run away from him? But that's precisely how mainstream environmentalists are dealing with climate change. For the life of me, I couldn't understand why anyone was taking them seriously.

The more I looked into climate change, the more depressed I got. I was swimming against the current which was so strong that I didn't think there was anything I could do to prevent humanity from committing suicide in short order. I plumbed the depths of that depression at SAI sanctuary in the Western Ghats of India.

There was nothing wrong with that sanctuary. In fact, I had the sense of perfection at the sanctuary as every tree, plant, animal, bird and insect just lived and the sanctuary thrived. I was in awe of the perfection of nature as a systems design. I asked Pamela, the owner of SAI Sanctuary,

"How did you make this happen?"

She replied,

"We bought a coffee plantation, tore down the fences and gave it back to the animals. They did everything. They dropped seeds and new trees were born."

"Wow, that's all you had to do to bring the forest back?"

"Well, we had to do one more thing. We had to patrol the land and make sure that no human beings came inside!"

At that point, I felt really, really small as if I didn't even belong in my own home. I was born in that forest, just 200Km away from where I was standing, nearly five decades ago.

Were humans the only species that don't belong on Earth? If we take humans out, the planet thrives. When humans are added to the mix and lead their ordinary lives, the planet dies.

That's such a depressing story to tell about ourselves.

Later during that trip to SAI Sanctuary, I observed an elephant tearing branches off a tree, eating the leaves and throwing the branches away. I asked Pamela,

"Isn't that elephant destroying your sanctuary?"

She replied,

"No, wherever the elephant tears branches off trees, the sunlight streams down through that opening to nourish the underbrush. Without the elephant doing that, the forest canopy would be so thick that the underbrush would die. In fact, the elephant has no choice but to be in alignment with nature."

She confirmed to me once again that all other species are routinely aligned with nature, while Homo Sapiens is the only species that don't belong on Earth.

The next year, our granddaughter, Kimaya was born. I was living in California at that time, while she was born in Arizona. I went to see her when she was a month old, held her in my arms for the first time and she looked up at me and smiled. Kimaya has the genetic mix of three continents, Asia, Africa and North America and I had the feeling that I was holding all of humanity in my arms. Her smile was a dazzling, knowing smile, as if she was saying,

"What do you mean I don't belong on Earth? I belong exactly as I am. You just haven't understood me yet."

I realized that this was the most amazing thing to have ever happened to me. I had to now rethink everything, assuming that humans are part of the same perfection of nature. I had to find a story in which humans belong exactly as we are, warts and all.

The answer was staring me in the face all along. As soon as we admit that humans possess the enormous power to change the climate of the planet, we automatically own the enormous responsibility to stabilize it and maintain it on behalf of all creation. We had been unknowingly HEATing the climate of the Earth for the past ten thousand years at least. By doing so, we prevented the Earth from going back to another ice age. Now it is well past time for us to transform and consciously begin healing the climate.

As Gus Speth said,

> "Thirty years ago, I thought that the three major environmental problems were biodiversity loss, ecosystem collapse and climate change. And I thought that with thirty years of good science, we can solve these problems.
>
> I was wrong.
>
> The three major environmental problems are selfishness, greed and apathy. To solve these problems, we need a spiritual and cultural transformation. And we scientists don't know how to do that."

It required divine intervention instead.

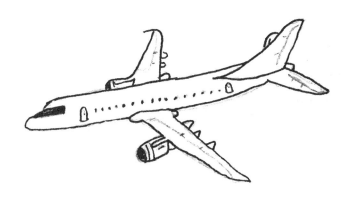

move to Phoenix

Chapter 2
The Move to Phoenix

I began to see Kimaya regularly over the next year and a half before we moved permanently to Phoenix in 2012 to be close to her. Sri Aurobindo had said that prison life had taught him to see Lord Krishna in the jailers and in every rat. I was seeing Lord Krishna very clearly in Kimaya.

"Yada-yada hi dharmasya
Glanir bhavati bharata
Abhyuthanam adharmasya
Thadatmanam srijamy aham

Paritranaya sadhunam
Vinashaya cha dushkritam
Dharma-samsthapanarthaya
Sambhavami Yuge Yuge"

—

"Whenever, O Bharata, righteousness declines
And unrighteousness takes hold, I manifest myself.

I manifest myself from time to time to defend the pious,
Destroy the wicked and strengthen righteousness."

A year prior to Kimaya's birth, I had encountered Mr. Jani in Chicago, who had held my head in his hands, put one thumb on the center of my forehead and another at the back of my head and said,

"This is Lord Krishna talking to you through me. Your inspiration comes through here (pressing the back of my head) and your execution comes through here (pressing the center of my forehead). Do your work without any ego and let me do it through you."

While Mr. Jani's words ring true throughout the Bhagavad Gita, that Lord Krishna works through all of us, I was stunned that I felt Mr. Jani's thumb on my forehead for hours after he left. I still feel it every time I meditate.

As far as I am concerned, Kimaya is the avatar manifested upon earth to lead us through the transformation from a Climate HEATing civilization to a Climate Healing civilization. There was nothing anyone could do to dissuade me otherwise.

I resolved that I was going to do whatever this baby girl wanted, whenever she wanted it. If she wanted me to jump, I was going to jump. If she wanted me to dance, I was going to dance.

That resolution turned Kimaya into the greatest teacher that I ever had in my life. She not only turned my head around 180 degrees to see humans as an integral part of nature, she also helped me unlearn the falsehoods and violence that had been deeply ingrained in me through my cultural upbringing.

All I had to do was to let her lead and follow along with my eyes wide open. I tried to understand reality from her innocent perspective.

The truth shall set you free, indeed.

HEAT is Human Earth Animal Torture.

HEAL is Human Earth Animal Liberation.

To liberate ourselves from our Climate HEATing civilization and create a Climate Healing civilization, we must let a little child in our life lead us.

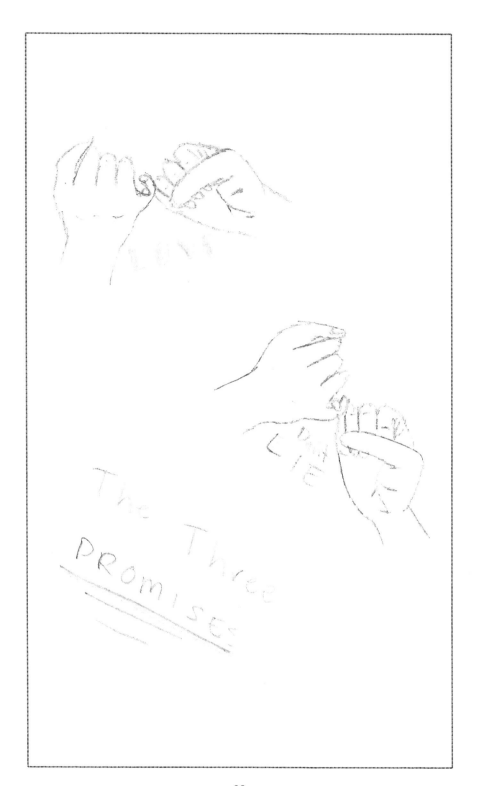

The Three
PROMISES

Chapter 3
The Three Promises

Life with Kimaya as the boss of my world was so much fun. She wanted to play with me whenever she came over to our home.

We played catch.

We played hide and seek.

We played chutes and ladders.

We hiked together on the desert trails around our home.

We played "Thenkela Pujela," a rocking game that my grandfather had taught me. It goes like this:

"Thenkela Pujela
Tharaikku Neerpondu
Athaneku Neerpondu
Southekaiku Neerpondu

Anchina Pole
Inchina Pole
Dum, dum, dum,
Dum, DUM!"

It is a Tulu song that speaks of water flowing here and there, nourishing trees and plants and ends with a coconut falling from the tree. To illustrate this, I would lie down on the ground, put Kimaya on my feet and rock her back and forth, left and right and then lift her up and let her fall into a big hug on my chest.

She loved that the most and constantly asked me to do that with her.

When she was about two years old, I made three promises to her to lay the foundations for our relationship:

1. She is the most amazing thing that ever happened to me and that will never, ever change,
2. I will always love her no matter what she does from now on, and
3. I will always tell her the truth and I will never, ever lie to her.

I made that third promise because I had found out that I had been lied to as a child, in my school textbooks, for heaven's sake! The protein myth and the calcium myth are still routinely drilled into children's heads even though adults ought to know that they are lying to children.

I consider lying to children to be a crime against humanity. I wish we lived in a society that didn't commit such crimes.

A couple of years after I made these three promises, Kimaya came to me and asked,

"Grandpa, are you sure that in your whole entire life, I am the most amazing thing that ever happened to you?"

I replied,

"Kimaya, that is the only thing I am really sure of."

Tag

Catch

Hide n' seek

Thenkela pujela

Infinite
GAMES

Chapter 4
Infinite Games

Kimaya didn't like games in which there were winners and losers, unless she always won. She preferred games that went on forever - infinite games - until she decided to play something else.

One time, when we were playing hide and seek, she came to me and said,

"I don't like it when I can't find you. From now on, I am going to tell you where to hide."

And then she would pretend to look for me elsewhere until she decided to "find" me. It wasn't the finding that she was interested in, it was just playing the game.

When we played catch around the kitchen center island, I, in the spirit of her liking for infinite games, pretended never to be able to catch her until she finally stopped. That worked until she was about five years old. After that, I really couldn't catch her as the turning radius of the center island was so sharp that she could go around it faster than me.

Kimaya's preference for infinite games extended to chutes and ladders, a board game that she loved to play. She would decide to go down a ladder or go up a chute or go straight from finish to home so that the game doesn't end at all until she would get bored with it.

In our Climate HEATing civilization, we tend to play finite games in which there is one winner and all others are "losers." In the Climate Healing civilization that we are called to create now, we should be playing infinite games, where the object of the game is to continue the game forever.

After all, that is what sustainability is all about. We want to thrive on this planet forever, don't we?

Chapter 5
What is Wrong With King Dasaratha?

My relationship with Kimaya was that of a devotee to an avatar. I did whatever she wanted and I respected all her views.

I was proud of our Hindu epics, the Ramayana and the Mahabharata, and I found children's versions of these epics to read to her in bed.

However, before I could get through even the first chapter of the Ramayana, she stopped me sternly and said,

"What is wrong with King Dasaratha?"

I was puzzled. I asked,

"What do you mean?"

"Why is he shooting a deer? That deer was just drinking water from the river and he goes and shoots it? What is wrong with him?"

And then she said,

"Don't ever read stories like these to me again."

That was the end of the epics as far as she was concerned. She didn't want to hear about violence towards animals even if it was meant to be taken symbolically.

Chapter 6
The Cinderella Principles

The Lily James version of Cinderella was released in 2015 when Kimaya was just 4 years old. One day after the release, I was babysitting her and she insisted that I take her to see the movie right away.

I agreed. I thought I would be bored watching yet another remake of the familiar story. However, within the first ten minutes of the movie, I sat up and started paying close attention when Cinderella said,

"Have courage, be kind and all will be well."

That simple statement captured in a nutshell what everyone should do if we wish to thrive on this planet. It takes courage to be kind when others are routinely cruel around you.

I realized at that point that this movie was for me and not just for her.

Cinderella made two other statements that form the basis of our work at Climate Healers. She said,

"Just because it is what is done doesn't mean that it is what should be done."

Just because we have been doing something all along doesn't

mean we should continue doing it. It is our responsibility to question our culture and traditions and renew them every now and then.

The last statement was,

"Imagine the world as it should be and act for it."

Imagine the world that you want and work for it, instead of going along with the world as it is.

I included these three Cinderella principles in my presentation at the European Union parliament later that year to much ovation. They form the cornerstone of our work at Climate Healers.

the LABYRINTH

PLEASE SEE
the
OBVIOUS!

Chapter 7
Consciousness is in Everything

Kimaya saw emotions and feelings not just in everyone, but also in everything. Once she accompanied me to give a lecture on climate change at a library in Prescott, Arizona, two hours from our home in Phoenix. She patiently sat through the lecture and then we returned home.

Once home, I discovered that I had forgotten the power adapter for my laptop at the library. I tend to use devices until they literally stop working and therefore, my laptop was quite useless without a power adapter as the battery couldn't hold much charge.

I was debating whether to go back to Prescott and pick up my power adapter, a 4 hour round trip, or to buy a substitute in Phoenix for $20. I asked Kimaya what I should do.

Her reply was immediate,

"Grandpa, you have to go back and get it from the library. That power adapter must be sad that it is not with the laptop."

And that's what we did. We spent four hours driving back and forth because in her view, emotions and feelings are in everything, not just everyone. This is in alignment with the Vedantic worldview that consciousness is in everything.

Later that year, I was returning back from the UN Climate Change meeting in Paris, France when I encountered a couple and their two children at the international airport. The husband was on his phone and walked off onto an inclined moving escalator, while the mother was standing at the foot of the escalator with a roll-on bag, a baby carriage with their infant son and their daughter, who seemed to be about Kimaya's age. She asked me,

"Sir, can you please help me?"

I replied,

"Of course. Would you like me to take the bag for you?"

She said,

"No, can you please hold my daughter through the escalator."

I held her daughter by the hand and stepped on the escalator. At that moment, I felt the same outpouring of love and affection that I normally feel when I hold Kimaya by the hand. There was absolutely no difference.

From that point on, I became conscious that every child in the world is my grandchild and that I'm working to heal the climate for all of them, not just Kimaya.

The Kindergardin
VISITY

Would eat YOU
deliberatly hurt
an
animal?

42

Chapter 8
The Kindergarten Class Visit

As a present, Kimaya received a necklace with the word, "Vegan" written on it. When she got it, she asked me if I would come to her Kindergarten class and explain to her friends what "Vegan" means. I told her that if her teacher allowed it, I would be happy to do that.

She got permission from her teacher and I went to her class the next day. Her friends gathered around me and asked,

"What does 'Vegan' mean?"

I said,

"Imagine that a bunny rabbit hops into this room. How many of you would play with the rabbit?"
"Oh, we all would play with the rabbit!"

"How many of you would hurt the rabbit?"
"Oh, we would never hurt the rabbit!"

I said,

"Then, you are all Vegan. Vegan means that you wouldn't knowingly hurt innocent animals unnecessarily."

The children were elated.

Later that week, Jaine got a call from the Principal to tell me never to do that again. Apparently, the children went home and told their parents that they were all Vegan. The parents called the Principal to complain.

A few weeks later, Kimaya's teacher called me to ask if I would come back to class and talk about India. I agreed.

The Principal called Jaine and asked that I never mention the word Vegan in class. I agreed again.

I went to school with my laptop and was setting it up when the Principal walked into class. I was surrounded by the children and the only thing they wanted to talk about was Veganism and how their parents were not allowing them to be Vegan.

The Principal realized that there was nothing I could do about it. It was the children who wanted to talk about Veganism, not me.

A few months later, the Principal watched the documentary *What The Health* and turned Vegan as well.

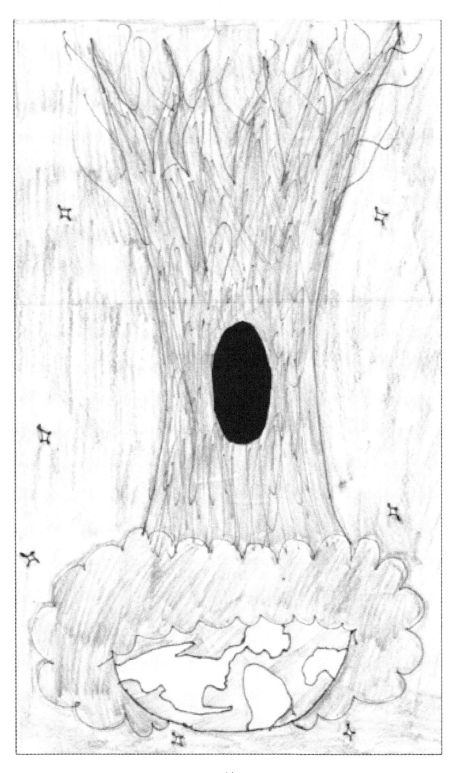

Chapter 9
The Story of the Wishing Tree

During my Kindergarten class visit, Kimaya asked me to tell her friends the wishing tree story. This was one of her favorite stories.

The story begins with children playing with sticks, stones and rag dolls on the floor of their hut in the middle of the forest. Their uncle comes to visit them and he says,

"Hey, why are you playing with sticks and stones when the wishing tree is right outside your hut? Go out under the tree and wish for anything you want and it will give it to you. Then you can be playing with real toys instead of just sticks and stones."

The children don't believe him. How can there be a tree that gives you anything you want?

They wait until the uncle leaves and then they rush to the tree and start wishing.

They wish for sweets and they get them. They gorge on the sweets and get stomach aches.

They wish for toys and they get them. They play with the toys and get bored.

They wish for fancier toys. That leads to greater boredom.

There was something about the tree that they did not understand. The tree grants you what you wish for and along with it comes the exact opposite.

The children didn't know that. All they knew is that they couldn't stop wishing under the tree and the more they wished, the more miserable they were.

Then they get to be young men and women and now they are wishing for what young men and women wish for. They get their wishes along with their opposites. They are now even more miserable.

Then they become old men and women. They gather under the tree in three different groups. The first group says,

"We were so happy when we didn't know about this tree. This has all been a hoax and a farce."

They were fools for they understood nothing about the tree.

The second group says,

"We must have been wishing for all the wrong things. If we could go back and wish for different things, we would have been a lot happier."

They were bigger fools for they understood less than nothing about the tree.

The third group was the most foolish of the lot for they say,

"We are so miserable that we wish we were dead."

The tree grants them the wish and they are immediately reborn underneath the tree for it always grants wishes along with their opposites.

Meanwhile, a lame child was watching all this from inside the window of the hut. He also wanted to go out under the tree and wished for a good leg so that he could walk properly, but there was such a crowd of people under the tree that he couldn't get through.

He stood there and he watched and he saw how the tree was making everybody miserable. The people who were wishing were miserable. Those who were trying to get to the tree were miserable. And all the animals were suffering because of all the wishing.

Then he had a flash of insight. He understood the tree. With that understanding, he began to feel a well of compassion come from within him for all the suffering under the tree. He lost the desire to wish and became detached from the tree. He was perfectly happy with his leg as it was. And with that, he was the happiest of the lot.

The lame child's insight is this. The wishing tree makes you miserable if you wish for yourself. But if you wish for the benefit of others and ask for nothing from the tree for yourself, then you can be perfectly happy wishing under the tree and everyone would be happy because of your wishing.

The Sloth story

Chapter 10

The Story of the Sloths

It was frequently my job to put Kimaya to bed and I always read or told her a story until she dozed off. Since she couldn't stand violence towards anyone, I had to change common fairy tales to read them to her since almost all of them are violent.

But the best stories were the ones we made up. She loved stories about animals and of course, every animal had to be named. More often than not, she wanted one of the animals named after herself.

Her all time favorite story is the one we made up about the Sloth family. It goes like this:

A family of sloths, Papa Sloth, Mama Sloth and Baby Sloth were living up a tree in the forest. Every morning, Mama used to get up early in the morning and fetch breakfast for the baby. One morning, Mama was not feeling well and she woke up Papa and asked if he would fetch breakfast for the baby.

He said,

"All right."

And off he went sleepily. But instead of going this way, he went that way. He returned later with a pear and handed it to Baby.

Baby said,

"What is this?"

Papa said,

"It's a pear."

"But Mama always brings me a mango for breakfast. I don't want a pear."

Mama said,

"Which way did you go? There was a mango tree nearby if you went this way."

"Well, I went that way."

Baby started whining,

"Please bring me a mango for breakfast. I don't want to eat a pear!"

Papa said,

"OK, but it's going to take me 6 hours. 1 hour to climb down from this tree, 1 hour to get to the mango tree, 1 hour to climb up the mango tree and then double it all for the trip back."

Baby was shocked,

"What, six hours?? Six HOURS!!!

Oh, all right, just give me the pear, I'll eat it."

Kimaya would laugh out loud. She never got tired of this story.

Unity Stew

Chapter 11

The Unity Stew

Kimaya liked to help me cook. She cut vegetables, ground up spices, washed the rice or lentils and even poured the idlis at times. But above all, she loved to stir the pot when we were making soup.

She loved her vegetable soup. We used to make it with potatoes, carrots, greens and a hearty onion, tomato and ginger base. Then she asked me to add beans. She loved that bean and vegetable soup garnished with dill.

After eating this bean and vegetable soup a few times, she asked me to add pasta or some grains. At that point, I realized that we had created a complete meal, a stew not just a soup.

We experimented with various bean, grain, vegetable and herb combinations. The result is the Unity Stew recipe template:

Ingredients
- **2 cups cooked legumes** (red/black/pinto beans or lentils)
- **2 cups mixed vegetables**, cut and cubed (typically potatoes, carrots, celery, sweet potatoes, squash, pumpkin, etc.)
- **1 cup grains** (whole grain pasta, brown rice, barley etc.)
- **1 medium onion**
- **1 tomato**
- **Juice of 1 lime or lemon**
- **½ inch stick of ginger**
- **1 cup chopped herbs and greens** (rosemary, thyme, cilantro, spinach, kale, chard, etc.)
- **salt and spices**, to taste
- **½ tsp turmeric powder**
- **pinch of asafetida**
- **4 cups water**

Recipe

Puree onion, tomato and ginger into a paste.

Bring water to boil, add cut vegetables, onion-tomato-ginger paste, turmeric, lemon juice, asafetida, spices and salt. *(The ginger and asafetida serve to alleviate "gasiness" from the beans and lentils.)* Simmer until vegetables are cooked.

Add cooked beans, herbs and greens, and grains. Simmer for 10 minutes or until grains are cooked. Set stew to cool.

Makes about 5 servings.

This is the stew that is being served at Food Healers stations today. It fills you up and heals you, which is the first thing we all need to do, if we wish to collectively heal the planet. This is the "put on your own mask first before helping others" oxygen mask rule: we need to take care of each other and heal ourselves first before helping the planet to heal.

When I look around me, I see rich, unhealthy, overfed people or poor, unhealthy, underfed people. It's as if our species is the only one that doesn't know how to feed itself, even though we are taking six times as much food as we need from the planet. Of course, we do know that whole-foods, plant-based Vegan eating would not only heal our species, but also return enough land and the ocean back to nature to heal the planet.

During the COVID-19 pandemic, Kimaya and I began cooking up versions of this Unity Stew and serving it to those who had lost their jobs in Phoenix, for free. Then it occurred to me that if a community can always provide healthy food for free to its members, that community would escape the clutches of its enslavement and heal itself.

It is time to make this happen across all communities around the world. That would signal our intent to address climate change seriously. The Unity Stew was the genesis of Food Healers and World Food Healers day that was first celebrated on November 19, 2022, Kimaya's 12th birthday.

Chapter 12
The Pinky Promise

From the outset of my work at Climate Healers, I was watching the loss of wild animals as the leading indicator for how fast we need to transform from a Climate HEATing civilization to a Climate Healing civilization. This is because everything we do to the environment impacts wild animals.

We pollute their water and take away their habitats, mainly to grow our domestic animals. Our domestic animals now consume more than 10 times as much food as all the wild animals did 10,000 years ago. As a result, wild animals are dying off exponentially.

The World Wildlife Fund has been documenting the loss of wild animals since 1970. Their Living Planet Reports are published every two years and report statistics on the loss of wild animals with a four year time lag. LPR 2014 reported that the wild animal population decreased by 52% between 1970 and 2010.

When that report came out in 2014, I worked out that if the loss of wild animals was proportional to the size of the global economy, we were on track to wipe out almost 100% of wild animals by 2026. I was shocked by that calculation, but hesitated to raise a public alarm about it because my model was truly crude.

I waited for the next report. LPR 2016 came out in Aug 2016 and it stated that the wild animal population decreased by 58% between 1970 and 2012.

I was numb with grief and regret. Why did I wait two years to raise the alarm? My earlier calculations were spot on.

That night, I was reading Ruby Roth's storybook *That's Why We Don't Eat Animals* to Kimaya in bed. At the end of the story, she put her head on my shoulder and said,

"Grandpa, who were the first human beings?"

Now, that's a very deep question that's difficult to answer truthfully. I thought about how I could explain Darwin's scientific theory to a five-year-old girl. Then I said,

"Imagine that you are standing on the street and holding your mama by your hand. You ask your mama to bring her mama to stand by her side. And so on, so that you create a long line of mothers on this side of the street.

On the other side of the street, you ask a chimpanzee to do the same thing with her mother, her grandmother and so on.

By the time these two lines go from Phoenix to Tucson, they would merge. Because both lines are going to say, 'Hey, that's my mama too!'"

Kimaya sat up in bed immediately. She said,

"WHAT?? Are you telling me that animals are my family?"

I replied,

"Now that you put it that way, yes they are your family."

Until then, I knew the scientific theory of evolution, but hadn't put it together like that. For her, "Vasudhaiva Kutumbakam" or "All life is one family" became visceral. Then, she started bawling her eyes out,

"Why are people eating my family? Grandpa, make them stop, make them stop! They are eating my family!"

She started naming names of people she knows who were eating her family. I realized that in keeping my promise to always tell her the truth, I had created a world full of monsters for my precious grand-daughter. Perhaps, every child goes through this phase at some point in their life.

I was grief-stricken. My heart was being wrenched out of my chest hearing her cries. I tried to console her,

"Kimaya, please don't cry. I'm working on it. In fact, it's my job to make them stop."

She stopped crying and looked at me wide eyed,

"WHAT? This is your job? This is your job? You know you haven't done your job!"

Then she shook her finger in my face — "DO YOUR JOB!"

And followed it up with,

"When will you do your job?"

I blurted out,

"I better do it by 2026 or else we are going to be in big trouble."

She said,

"Will you promise me that?"

"Sure, I'll promise you that."

"Will you give me a pinky promise?"

I had no idea what a pinky promise meant. I said,

"OK, I'll give you a pinky promise."

She told me to hold out my pinky, locked her pinky in mine and said,

"You can never ever break a pinky promise."

Then she put her head on my shoulder and went to sleep.

And I couldn't sleep. I realized that I had made a very serious promise to a little girl on behalf of my generation and I better figure out how to keep it.

I finally dozed off and woke up knowing that as a systems engineer, I'm uniquely qualified to take on the responsibility for creating a Vegan World by 2026.

Later on, the Climate Bathtub model that I created for the UN COP26 climate change meeting in Glasgow confirmed that at a bare minimum, the world needs to go largely Vegan by 2026 if we wish to avert runaway climate change as well.

As an engineer, I deal with probabilities, not certainties. I know that the odds are not good for a soft landing for our Climate HEATing civilization. However, we are called to be Captain Sullenbergers in this possible "Miracle on the Hudson" moment for our civilization.

Captain Sullenberger told his passengers and crew to "Brace for Impact," and miraculously landed his US Airways plane with 155 passengers on the Hudson river in 2009 even after his plane's engines had been accidentally killed by a flock of migrating Canadian geese. Following his fine example, Food Healers are calling for free, healthy whole foods, plant based Vegan meals for all, regardless of their race, color, creed or nation so that we may envelope our fellow humans with love as we do our best to create a soft landing for this Climate HEATing civilization. In the process, we can also prepare the infrastructure and institutions for a Climate Healing civilization to take its place.

Faith and action are the best antidotes for apathy and despair.

This is how Kimaya taught me what to do, how to do it and gave me a timeline for doing my job at Climate Healers. I think that she did more by the time she turned six to solve climate change than all the world's governments combined.

May a little child in your life help you find the inspiration to do your part in our ongoing transformation from a Climate HEATing civilization to a Climate Healing civilization.

I'm apprehensive but also excited to be participating in this Greatest Transformation in Human History as it unfolds over the next few years with all of you, my amazing fellow human beings!

Please HELP us —

Heal the planet.
Eat plants.
Love animals.
Plant trees.

Yes, it's that simple.

*"... until we see
the obvious and
stop hiding behind
culture, we won't
solve the problem."*

- Glen Merzer

Epilogue

The Creator Checks in on Earth — By Glen Merzer

Let's imagine what would happen if the Creator came back to visit Earth and had a few minutes to point out what we're doing wrong. Let's say She met with the head statistician of the UN who knows everything we're doing on the Earth. Here's how that dialogue might go.

—

CREATOR: Well, you know I haven't checked in on the Earth for 50,000 years. I was always very proud of the beautiful blue-green Earth and also very proud of you human beings. Way back in the beginning, you were already developing big brains and I predicted great things from you.
But I understand there's been a problem and you've been overheating the Earth with too much greenhouse gases?

UN GUY: Yeah, we have more carbon dioxide in the atmosphere every year. We're approaching unsustainable levels. We have more deadly storms and fires and heat. Pretty soon we won't be able to breathe.

CREATOR: I remember that I created six trillion trees that drink carbon dioxide, so what seems to be the problem?

UN GUY: Well, six trillion trees would have solved the problem, but we don't have six trillion trees anymore; we just have three trillion.

CREATOR: You mean to say that you lost three trillion trees? How did you do that? Is that because of this coal industry that I have heard about?

UN GUY: Well, actually the coal industry hasn't cost us that many trees. Sometimes we dig up a mountain. It doesn't look very nice and we lose some trees, but not much. So our tree loss is not because of the coal industry.

CREATOR: Well, is it because of the oil industry? Is that what's causing all that tree loss?

UN GUY: No, the oil industry doesn't cost us that many trees. Sometimes we have oil spills. We had a terrible spill in the Gulf of Mexico a few years ago with many millions of barrels of oil pouring into the water.

CREATOR: It comes out in barrels?

UN GUY: No, but that's how we like to think of it.

CREATOR: Well, that must've been very bad for the fish. I remember that I created a whole lot of fish.

UN GUY: No, actually, it was good for the fish. When we had the big oil spill, a lot of the fish came back.

CREATOR: That's odd. I remember that when I created fish, they didn't drink oil. Why did you wind up with more fish when you spilled oil into the gulf?

UN GUY: You see, when the oil spill happened, we humans stopped fishing, so that brought back the fish. The fish may not like oil, but they like oil a lot better than they like us.

CREATOR: Wait a minute. Hold on here! I remember that I created you to live in the forests. I created you as land animals—cousins to the apes, chimps, and gorillas. Do chimps and gorillas eat fish?

UN GUY: No, of course not.

CREATOR: So why do you people eat fish?
UN GUY: Well, it's part of our culture.

CREATOR: Culture? I don't remember creating culture.
UN GUY: You didn't. We did.

CREATOR: What's the purpose of culture?
UN GUY: The purpose of culture is to proudly carry on doing things from one generation to the next even when we know they are wrong.

CREATOR: What kind of things do people proudly carry on doing because of culture?
UN GUY: Oh, cultures have given us art and music and dance as well as, you know, some other stuff on the violent side like slavery, racism, bullfighting, fishing, and raising animals to kill them. Have you ever seen Irish step dancing? It is terrific.

CREATOR: So, because of your culture, you've been eating fish? What has this done to the oceans?
UN GUY: Oh, we're destroying all the oceans because we eat fish.

CREATOR: All the oceans? That's about 70% of the earth!
UN GUY: Give or take. They're getting bigger now because of global warming.

CREATOR: How much of your food do you get from fish?
UN GUY: About 3% of our food.

CREATOR: So, you've destroyed all of the oceans to get just 3% of your food? How many fish do you kill every year?
UN GUY: Oh, trillions of them. We kill a lot more than we eat, because that's how nets work. The nets also kill dolphins and whales, which aren't technically fish. And we kill and eat lobsters and crabs, which also aren't fish. Anything in the ocean is fair game. We feed a lot of the fish to cows. Cows eat more fish than we do.

CREATOR: I don't remember creating cows.

UN GUY: Right, you created oxen but we kind of fattened them up and softened them up and turned them into cows to make them taste better.

CREATOR: So how many cows do you have now? Do you have hundreds of these cows?

UN GUY: We now have 1.5 billion cows. Eating them is part of our culture.

CREATOR: 1.5 billion? So how much of the Earth's land do cows take up?

UN GUY: We've turned over about 37% of the Earth's land to the cows and then another 6% we use to grow grain to feed to the cows.

CREATOR: Wait. Let me get this straight. You are using 43% of the Earth's land to grow cows?

UN GUY: That's right. They weigh about 1600 pounds each so they have to eat a lot of grass on top of the fish and the chicken manure and whatever else we can feed them.

CREATOR: You feed chicken manure to cows?

UN GUY: It's called recycling.

CREATOR: So 43% of the beautiful land on Earth is for the cows? Is that what happened to the 3 trillion trees?

UN GUY: Right, we had to chop down the 3 trillion trees and burn all the vegetation when we gave 43% of the Earth's land to the cows.

CREATOR: So I guess you must get most of your food from all these cows you eat and all the other animals you eat?

UN GUY: No, just 12%.

CREATOR: You're telling me you're destroying the planet I created in order to get only 12% of your food?

UN GUY: Plus the 3% from the fish, so to be fair, that's 15%

CREATOR: Have you no sense of shame?
UN GUY: I don't like to brag, but we've overcome it.

CREATOR: What happened to all the other animals I created on that land: tigers, leopards, giraffes, elephants?
UN GUY: Oh, we've been killing them. Between 1970 and 2016, we eliminated two-thirds of the ones that were left. We are on track to wipe out almost all of them by 2026.

CREATOR: And you do this because of this culture thing?
UN GUY: Yes, we do this because, you know, our culture revolves around eating animals. And hunting some we don't even eat.

CREATOR: Have you considered getting rid of culture?
UN GUY: Can't. The tourist industry depends on it. Every culture is a little bit different. People find that very charming. But most of them encourage us to eat cows.

CREATOR: I remember that I created you people to get hungry when you look at an apple. Do you get hungry when you look at a cow?
UN GUY: Of course not! Nobody gets hungry when they look at a cow!

CREATOR: Isn't that a clue?
UN GUY: Respectfully, you didn't create us to be a subtle species.

CREATOR: It's a little astonishing that you would turn over 43% of the land just to grow these cows that you eat.
UN GUY: We don't only eat them. We also drink their milk.

CREATOR: You've got to be kidding me? Baby humans drink the milk of cows?
UN GUY: Not just the babies. Adults, too.

CREATOR: You're pulling my leg?

UN GUY: I'm dead serious.

CREATOR: You are saying that fully grown humans– ?

UN GUY: Yes. Drink milk. And we turn it into all kinds of cheeses and get hooked on them.

CREATOR: Do you people have schools? Any education at all?

UN GUY: Yes, we do. And the textbooks in those schools are a proud part of our culture.

CREATOR: There we go again. And so I'll bet the text books teach you to eat cows and drink their milk?

UN GUY: You're catching on quick.

CREATOR: But doesn't it make you people fat and sick to eat 1600-pound animals and drink their milk?

UN GUY: You don't know the half of it. We spend all the money we make on doctors, and we fight about who should pay for it. There are some very big industries making a boatload of money off our diseases.

CREATOR: So why on Earth do you keep doing this?

UN GUY: I told you already.

CREATOR: Culture.

UN GUY: Right.

CREATOR: I was under the impression the last time I checked in on you that you were growing really big brains.

UN GUY: Yeah. Big enough to create culture. I guess not quite big enough to figure out what's wrong with it. We're kind of stuck in-between.

CREATOR: And now the Earth's atmosphere is overheating.

UN GUY: Yup.

CREATOR: And you like to tell each other that it's because of burning fossil fuels instead of the larger truth that it's because of what you've done to the oceans and to the land?

UN GUY: Yup. Because the fossil fuel industry isn't—

CREATOR: A big part of your culture.

UN GUY: Right. Nobody really celebrates gas stations. But food—

CREATOR: That's a big part of your culture.

UN GUY: Right. Can't question that.

CREATOR: Can't culture change? Do you still have slavery, racism, bullfighting?

UN GUY: We are working very hard to eradicate those things. We know they are wrong. I promise you that they will end, and soon.

CREATOR: Then promise me that you will end the culture of people eating animals and drinking their milk. I created you humans to protect the animals, not eat them. You need to change it, quick.

UN GUY: Change is hard for us. It takes us time.

CREATOR: You don't have much time because you are destroying the Earth, remember? Until you see the obvious and stop hiding behind culture, you won't solve the problem.

Listen to me now: the Earth is dying fast and I've got other worlds to check in on. You humans need to do your job, return the earth to the animals and the trees. Eat plants just like your cousins who are smarter than you think and would never dream of eating cows.

Let's get it done by 2026 and save the Earth.

Pinky Promise?

UN GUY: Pinky Promise!

—

So, I think that the Creator in a few minutes could help us understand that the burning of fossil fuels is a smaller part of the problem. The larger part is what we've done to the Earth. We've destroyed the oceans because we eat fish; we've destroyed the land and decimated the forests because we eat cows, which are not our food.

In the words of the Creator, until we see the obvious and stop hiding behind our culture, we won't solve the problem.

Sincerely,
Glen Merzer

—

Clean Plant Heal

Dump Dump Dump
Burn Burn Burn
Kill Kill Kill
The Climate is heating.
I wonder why...

Dump Dump Dump
Burn Burn Burn
Kill Kill Kill
The Arctic is melting.
I wonder why...

Dump Dump Dump
Burn Burn Burn
Kill Kill Kill
The Corals are bleaching.
I wonder why...

Dump Dump Dump
Burn Burn Burn
Kill Kill Kill
Our planet is dying.
I wonder why...

That's all more than enough to make Mother Earth cry.

Clean Clean Clean
Plant Plant Plant
Heal Heal Heal
Wow - Is the Climate cooling?
I think I know why.

Clean Clean Clean
Plant Plant Plant
Heal Heal Heal
Wow — is the Arctic freezing?
I think I know why.

Clean Clean Clean
Plant Plant Plant
Heal Heal Heal
Wow — are the Corals teeming?
I think I know why.

Clean Clean Clean
Plant Plant Plant
Heal Heal Heal
Wow — is the Earth healing?
I think I know why.

'Cause we banded together as one, do or die!

Acknowledgments

—

A book comes together with the collaboration of many devoted souls. I'm deeply indebted to Suzanne Ashley King for her beautiful layout and artistic input, Vivien Chinelli for cleaning up my amateurish poetic skills, Glen Merzer for contributing his brilliant one-act play, Judy McCoy Carman for contributing her inspiring Prologue, Suzanne McAllister and Anne Piotrowski for suggesting that I write this book in the first place, Jaine Rao for always being the rock in our family, Akhil Rao, Dolly Vyas-Ahuja and Pareen Sachdeva for putting up with me during our tour of India when this book got written and to that restaurant in Surat, Gujarat, India for giving me the brief respite from our hectic schedule that enabled me to write the book. Above all, I'm forever grateful to our precious granddaughter, Kimaya Rainy Rao, for turning my head around and making me see things in a whole new light.

I fervently pray that Kimaya and her generation will eventually forgive me and my generation for being so slow in seeing that light.

Made in the USA
Las Vegas, NV
28 January 2023

66379756R00049